Torina's World

Tantely tapa-bata ka ny foko no entiko mameno azy.

This is only half a pot of honey, but my heart fills it up.

—A Malagasy proverb

Torina's World
A Child's Life in Madagascar

Photographs and Text by
Joni Kabana

Edited by
Benjamin Opsahl

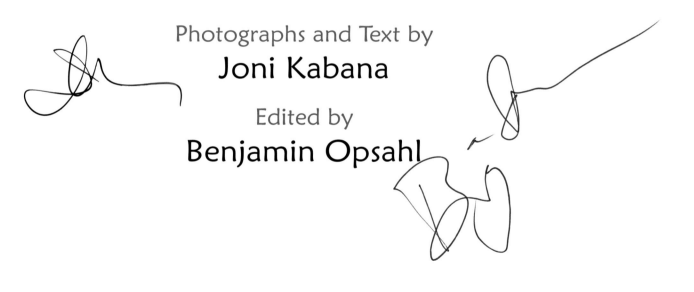

 arnica PUBLISHING, INC.
Portland, Oregon

This book is dedicated to each rapid heartbeat of discovery, to Torina,
for allowing me into her world, and to my children: Ben, Aaron and Brynn.

With special thanks to The Gonia Family for their patience, hospitality and trust while I was in Madagascar in 1996; to Michele and Marty for their caring support and encouragement, to Dennis Stovall and Barb Sanders for their ideas and consultation, and to Daniel Rakotoarijaona, Claudias Fidimanana, Mino Rakotoarijaona, Meredith Sorenson, Joshua Poole and Diana Skelton for their support while I was in Madagascar in 2007.

Our gratitude to Michael Hiles and Janey Place for making it possible for Torina's educational wish to come true.

A portion of the profits made from the sale of this book will be donated to non-profits with 501(c)(3) status. All inspired donations and kind actions of support can be offered via www.torinasworld.com or through the purchase of this book.

Library of Congress Cataloging-in-Publication Data

Kabana, Joni, 1956-
  Torina's world : a child's life in Madagascar / photographs and text by Joni Kabana ; edited by Benjamin Opsahl. -- 2nd ed.
    p. cm.
  ISBN 978-0-9794771-4-0 (alk. paper)
 1. Children--Madagascar--Social conditions--Juvenile literature. 2.
Madagascar--Social life and customs--Pictorial works--Juvenile literature.
3. Children--Madagascar--Pictorial works--Juvenile literature. I. Opsahl, Benjamin, 1988- II. Title.

HQ792.M3K33 2007
305.2309691--dc22

                           2007027780

Second edition ISBN: 978-0-9794771-4-0
First edition ©1997 Joni Kabana Photography, LLC—www.jkabana.com
Second edition © 2008 Joni Kabana
Photography by Joni Kabana
Cover and text design by Aimee Genter

Arnica Publishing, Inc.
3739 SE Eighth Ave, Suite 1
Portland, Oregon 97202
Phone: (503) 225-9900
Fax: (503) 225-9901
www.arnicacreative.com

Arnica books are available at special discounts when purchased in bulk for premiums and sales promotions, as well as for fund-raising or educational use. Special editions or book excerption can also be created for specification. For details, contact the Sales Director at the address above.

Foreword

Losing your place in our modern world is easy—just stop to think about how many superficial tasks you perform each day, and consider how many of them feel natural to you. With time, it can even become difficult to recall exactly what does feel natural.

Torina's World is a book about those little things we feel are natural. It will challenge the reader to think about how they live their lives. It is not just a children's book; while a child will enjoy the vibrant culture presented, adults will enjoy the refreshing minimalist and community-oriented perspective and will notice parallels to their own core values.

Creating the original Torina's World book was not easy—from the arduous initial trip my mother took to Malagasy villages, to the laborious initial start getting the book self-published. After plenty of hard work, collaboration, support from friends and family, and many late nights, the book was created for a very small audience in mind: our family. Ten years later, with worldwide focus shifting on preserving our natural ways of living, the message is more important than ever.

It is our hope that this book might bring a little something of its own to you—whether it be a smile, a shared memory with a loved one, or a new perspective on how you live your life—and that you will find a way to share your thoughts with others.

—Ben Opsahl

Introduction

The little girl you see on the cover of this book and in some of the photographs is named Torina. She helped me find many of the people in these photographs by taking me to small tribal habitats around the village of Marovoay in Madagascar. We did not understand each other's languages, but we talked with our eyes.

Many of the people in this book had never seen a camera before, and some of them had never seen a "vazaha," a foreigner. Some were excited and happy to see me; others were afraid and shy.

Torina learned how to use a camera. I learned how to see life differently.

Joni Kabana

Manakory! My name is Torina. I live in Madagascar.
Madagascar is a big island off the east coast of Africa in
the Indian Ocean. I live near lots of trees and I like to
pretend I am many things when I am around them.

Would you like to see some of the things we do in
Madagascar? I will show you …

We Live!

We make rice for supper every day.
What do you eat for supper?

We wash our clothes together.
How do you wash your clothes?

We grow food and sell it at the market.

Where do you get your food?

We make charcoal so we can cook our supper.
What things do you make?

We live in many kinds of houses.
What does your house look like?

We work together.

How do you work?

We take the taxi to the city.
Where do you go?

We get rides in the pousse-pousse.

What do you ride in?

We buy our cows from the market.

What do you buy at the market?

We rest together on our mat.
What do you do together?

We Grow!

We play outside.
Where do you play?

We take a bath.

How do you
take a bath?

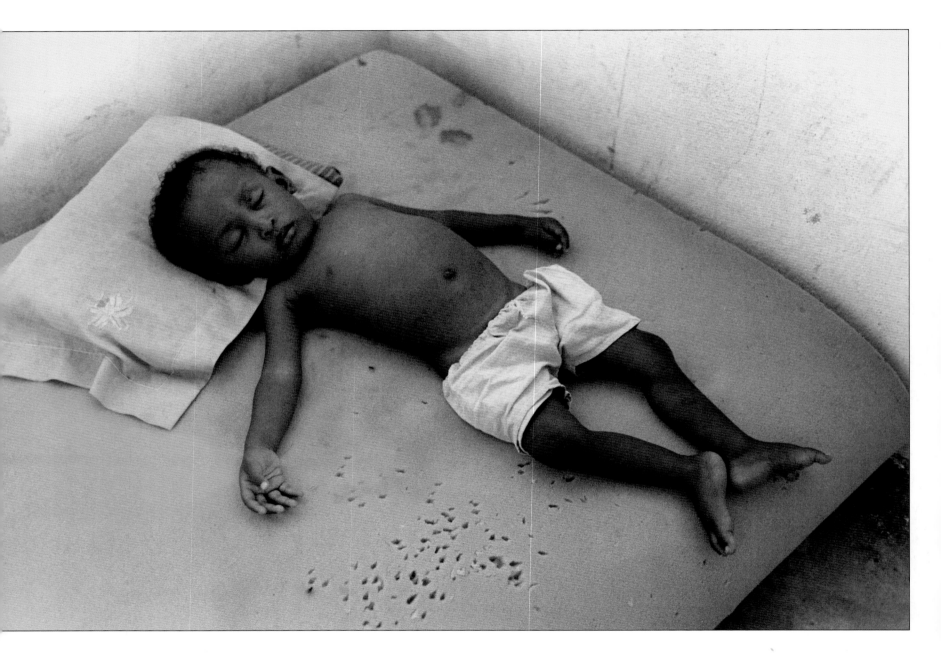

We sleep on our pillow.

Where do you sleep?

We carry our sisters and brothers.

What do you carry?

We love our brothers and sisters.

Who do you love?

We take care of each other.
What do you take care of?

We help our mothers.

Who do you help?

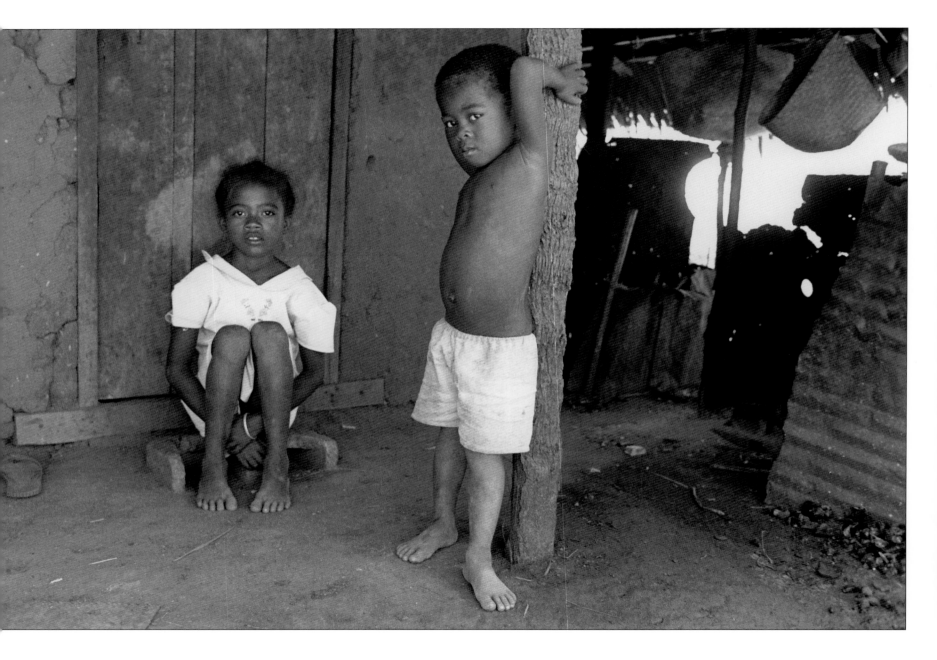

We wait by the kitchen.
What does your kitchen look like?

We look at ourselves in a photograph.

Do you have any photographs?

We play in the sea.

Where do you play in the water?

We see you!

Can you see us?

We dance!

How do you dance?

We play!

How do you play?

We Feel!

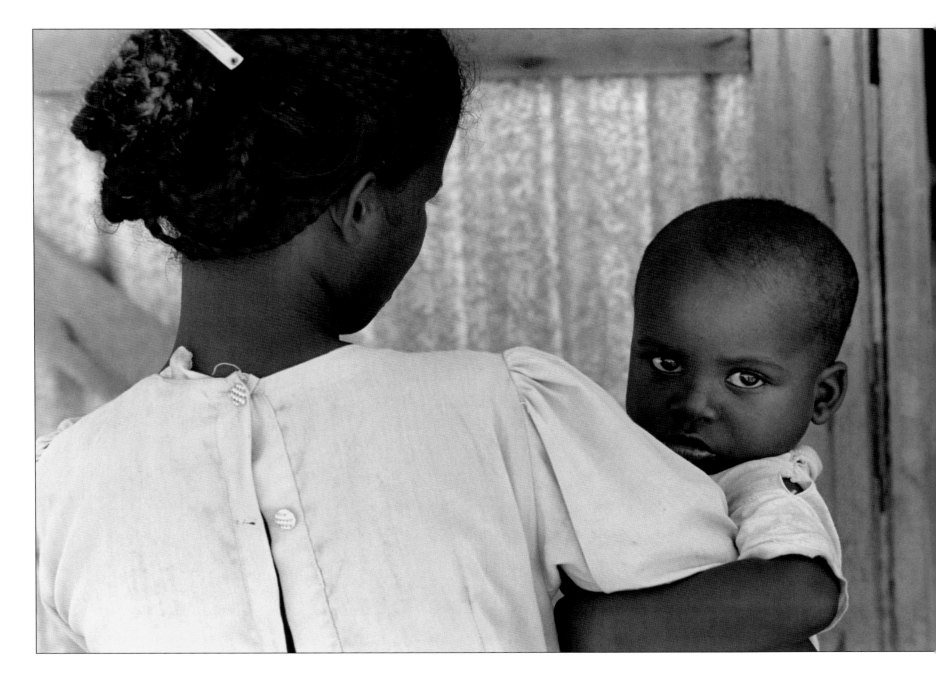

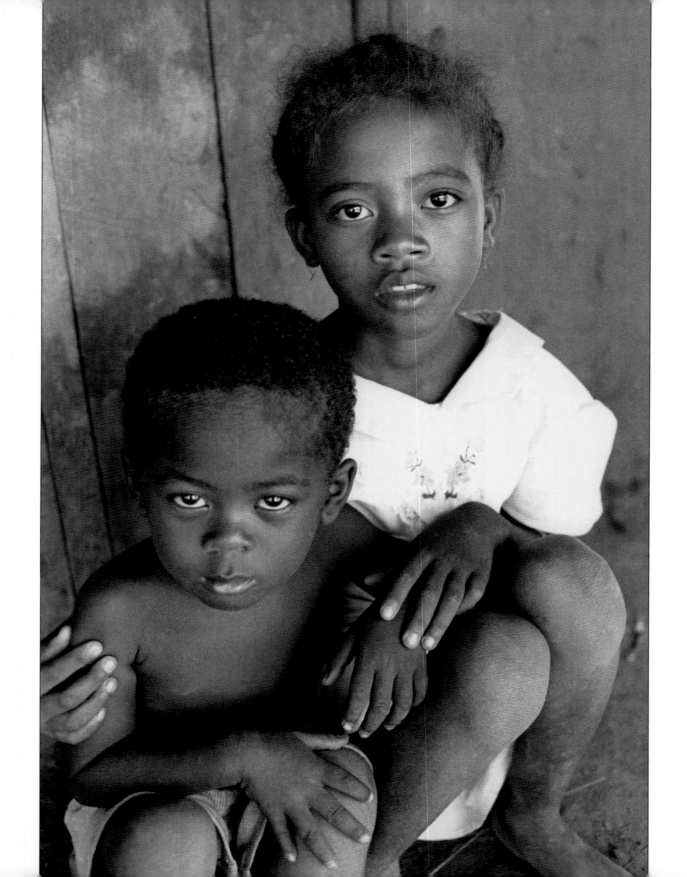

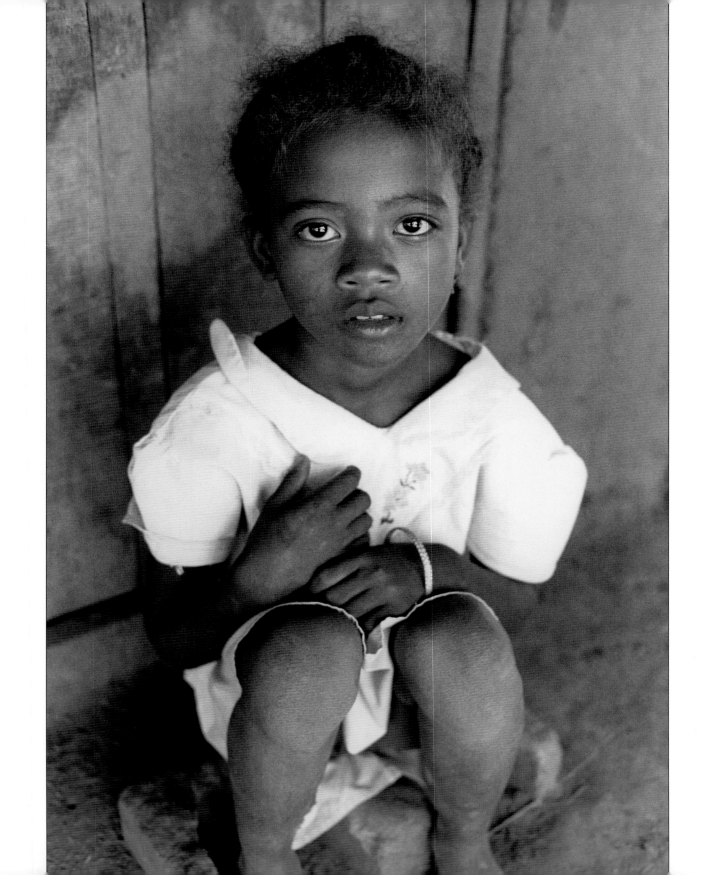

Madagascar is my home.

Where do you live?

Torina Today

Torina still lives in the small hut with her parents and seven brothers in a village near Marovoay, Madagascar. Her days consist mainly of fetching water, washing clothes at the river, cooking rice, and helping to care for her younger brothers. She walks approximately nine miles (three-and-a half hours each way) to get to school. She is at the top of her class, and is an extremely dedicated student. She has her heart set on becoming a doctor. A benefactor has paid for

the rest of her high school tuition, and we are planning additional fundraisers to help with her college expenses.

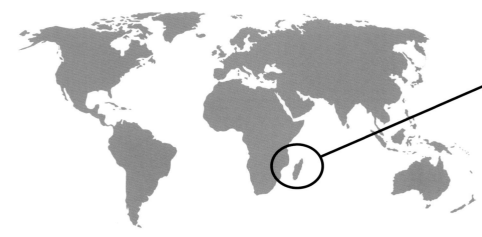

About Madagascar

Madagascar is the world's fourth largest island. Over 85 percent of this island's plants and animals are found only on this island and nowhere else on our earth. The island is 1,000 miles (1,580 kilometers) long by 350 miles (570 kilometers) wide.

The Malagasy people who live in Madagascar are very unique and have many beliefs. Most of them believe in their own way of ancestor worship, and some are Muslims, Hindus or Christians. Most of them live in one of eighteen different tribes.

The population is estimated at 19.5 million, nearly half of which are children under the age of fifteen. By the year 2025 the population is expected to exceed 30 million.

About the Author

After years as a technology executive, Joni Kabana quit her job to focus on her lifelong passion of photography. She is now a highly respected and award-winning Pacific Northwest commercial and portrait photographer. Her images of homeless children, cancer patients, and the "misunderstood," are hauntingly provocative. Joni was named "Compassionate Photographer of the Year" by Seattle's Rosewater Foundation and has been the recipient of various grants.

Ten years ago, Joni went to Madagascar to photograph other children and families as they went about their daily life. Her desire to bring international and diversity awareness to her own children motivated the trip and inspired the creation of the book. She says, "I love to see what is hidden within our preconceptions: the tenderness of a corporate executive, the fragility of a tough kid living on the streets, the wisdom in a child with cancer, the grace that simple living can instill." In 2007, she and her son, Ben, returned to see Torina again.

Joni resides in Portland, Oregon, but travels the world for her assignments.